# How to Get Good Tenants

**A Straight Forward Manual for Landlords on How to Get Good Tenants.**

> For your convenience we have designed some of the following information in two ways:
>
> (1) To the point information ..... ( no fluff )
> (2) Short narrative information. .... ( min. fluff )

© Copyright 2011

by:   *Michaelangelo Greco*

*aka  Michael  Greco*

# Table of Contents

## Disclaimer

**The following** are tips and guidelines for getting good tenants, Please, make certain that you know the  Fair Housing Law. Also note that Lease Agreements  and the   Rental Applications process  may be state sensitive,  therefore  please  check with a Lawyer for the appropriate requirements for your state.

**Important Notice**: The information herein contained is provided for your convenience and is meant as a guide to assist you.  Please note that any advice and/or information provided by us is not a substitute for the advice of an attorney and not meant to replace guidance from an attorney. **NO** representation or warranty as to legality, accuracy, correctness or acceptance of this said content by any State or jurisdiction is indicated.  We advise you to Counsel an attorney to ensure accuracy as each state and local laws vary.

# Introduction

One of the biggest challenges to a responsible landlord is getting good tenants.  In my years of experience I have talked with hundreds of landlords and many of them say the same thing:, " It's hard to find good tenants " and " How do you get good tenants? " .

Over the years I have successfully found great tenants, tenants I never wanted to leave, who loved the rental unit, cared for it, and paid their rent on time.  I've also experienced the opposite.  And with this experience I've learned the steps required to ensure that I get the best tenants for my rental units.  And now I want to share this knowledge with other landlords.  You need not feel alone.  This is why I created this manual " How to Get Good Tenants – A Straight Forward Manual With Minimum Fluff "

I say "Minimum Fluff" for a reason.  Your aren't going to read countless war stories, or situations.  What  I seek to present to the you the reader is a clear cut, easy to follow, instruction manual filled with detailed information on how landlords can get good tenants.

By reading, and more importantly, using the steps and guidelines presented on these pages landlords will learn how to prep their rental for the best renters, how to screen prospective tenants, and show their property in the most professional manner possible.

My hope is that you, as a landlord, will find easy guidance in this book, have greater income and the most success in finding and keeping good tenants.

# Chapter 1

**Location, Location, Location**, *It's easier to find a good tenant if your area is appealing and gives a good first impression.*

## Points

a.  **Demographics**: What is the demographics where your rental unit is located

b.  **Public Areas** : Are the public areas around your rental clean and well maintained ( Streets, Street Lights or Lamp Post, Sidewalks, Parks, Parking )

c.  **Public Amenities:** What amenities does the municipality offer such as bus, and bus hubs, trains, parks, to name a few.

d.  If you are investor looking to buy a rental property- observe the activity in the area after 5 pm or on the weekends ( most people are off from work) - a smart perspective renter will do the same.

- If some of the areas noted above are not up to par and are out of your personal control you may wish to contact your municipality or gather other property owners to create a better area.

- If your rental property is in a not so desirable area it's obvious it will be more difficult to find a good tenant. It may take more time and perseverance but they are out there.

**There are good locations in all income levels**. The old time tested saying in real estate is " Location, Location, Location, " In commercial real estate it is where a high volume of people frequent. This will usually have a high rent rate and should give you a good return on your investment ( as long as you buy right and secure a good tenant ). However with residential rentals it does not mean that it must be in a high volume area or be in the very expensive area. There are good rental locations in all income levels. The first step to a better return on investment for a residential rental property location is that the rental unit is in an appealing area.

1

# Chapter 2

**Curb Appeal** ,  *Your property is the first thing the prospective tenant looks at and gets a first  impression.  Make sure your property looks good, appealing and inviting*

a.   **Repair / Improvements**

- **Repair** any and every thing that is in need of repair or even looks broken.  Windows, Siding, Doors, Locks, Porch, Steps, Railings, Roof, or Paint.  If you are handy and can do some or all of the work needed than a little sweet equity will save some money.   If the work that is needed is out of your expertise then contact a licensed trades person or company to do the work. Get at least 3 bids and compare. Make sure the contractor is licensed and will give you a current certificate of insurance before the bid is accepted. Some of the following links can help to find an appropriate trades person in your area. Also, ask for a list of 5 references and check them. AngesList.com    contractor.com.

- **Exterior Paint**:  Where applicable, Exterior paint should last for many years however it could look bad after 3 or 4 year form winter grime.  A good spray wash in the spring will help keep the building looking fresh or paint just the front of the building if needed.

b.   **Front Entrance Door and Lanterns**

- **The Entrance door**  and Lanterns must look good. Depending on the type of door clean and shine or where applicable paint.  If the entrance finish is paint and just cleaning does not give the appearance of clean and new then **Paint the**  front door and trim. Sometimes a fresh coat ( a thin application of paint if using the same color )   or touch up of paint every 3 to 4 years may be needed.

- **Enhance the Look**: Depending on the style of your building you may want to enhance the door with color or trim.  If you need help with color and design call a professional, look through books and magazines for ideas (this is a great source of inspiration and ideas ) or sometimes a paint store may have its own design specialist.  By enhancing your front door it will not only add to the appearance and sometime change the look and feel of your property but also it will make a great first impression.

- **The lantern(s)** should coordinate with the look and style of you building and entrance area. It does not cost much to change the look by changing the lanterns. Sometimes when showing the property to a prospective tenant turn on the lanterns and let them glow. This not only adds to the ambience but also it give a warm, welcoming, and comfortable feeling.

c. **Clean and trim**

- Is your yard or lot clean, landscaped, well maintained, and appealing?

- **Clean** the yard or lot, landscape if needed, trim trees and shrubs, cut the grass and clean the trash area. It is important the yard or lot is well maintained and appealing. In addition to the above some edging around the sidewalk will also have a positive effect.

d. **Flowers, Shrubs, Potted Plants**.

**Spruce up the outside.** Planting low-maintenance bushes and flowers at the entrance area will make the rental look inviting. It also shows the landlord cares about the property. It is also great for pictures when marketing the property.

# Chapter 3

## Prepare Rental for Occupancy *People are attracted to nice surroundings and will feel good about themselves.*

**Points** Note:  The following points are steps that should be completed in the sequence  presented.

### Make it Attractive

a.  Fix,

- Any and everything that is broken or damage *must* be fixed and in good repair.

b.  Improvements or Updates

- **Kitchen appl. and fixtures**.  Should be cleaned to look like new inside and out and be in good working order.  Dirty appliances and fixtures will turn a good tenant off.  It will also leave a not so good impression on you as a landlord.

- If the appliances or fixtures are old and rundown they should be replaced.  Note: if you are replacing any fixtures spend a little extra to get a nice looking appliance or fixtures. It will be worth it and go a long way to getting a good tenant.

- **The bathroom and kitchen** are the two most important rooms in a rental unit a prospective renter will judge. By **spending a little extra** to get the nicer fixtures and new appliances if needed ( new appliances with basic or standard features and a low cost ) with some upgrades to make both the kitchen and bathroom look attractive will be well worth the investment.   Remember most people make decisions based on emotions. So If you can make the kitchen and bathroom " attractive "  you will certainly find some emotions in a prospective tenant.  It's a great feeling when you have many people who would like to rent where you need to select the best qualified applicant to rent to.

- Noted improvements will not only make your rental look great but it will also allow you to get a better rent and increase the value of your property. This will help if you ever decide to sell or refinance

later as it will contribute to the increased resale value of your property.

c.  **Paint**

- Some people like to use a flat paint and some use a semi-gloss paint because it is easier to clean. Either way if the walls can't be cleaned without it looking smudged it would be best to paint the walls.  Not only will the walls look good and the room(s) appealing but the smell of paint usually gives the impression of NEW and FRESH.

- When ordering paint get a little extra and store it in a safe place away from a flame or furnace. Also make sure the cans are sealed properly.  The extra paint can be used later for touch-ups and will save you the time and expense of painting the entire wall or walls at a later date especially when you are renting again.

- Before you store the extra paint it would be wise to make a note on each can of paint stating the apartment address / the room the paint was used in and the year it was painted.  This will be a great help later when you need to touch up.

- Rental properties should be painted using neutral colors. This will enable the tenant to match most any type of furniture and accessories.

d.  **Clean**

- After all of the Repairs and Improvements have been completed, if any were needed, then clean, clean, clean. If the rental unit is dirty or with clutter here and there a prospective good tenant will be turned off and most likely ex your rental. To begin cleaning start with the walls and windows then bedrooms, living room and dining room. Clean the bath and kitchen last. Cleaning in this order will help eliminate double work.   When doing the kitchen and bath " *Detail Clean* " and make sure that the everything **shines.** Wax the floors if needed.  It is worth mentioning again that the bathroom and kitchen are the two most important rooms in a rental unit a prospective renter will judge. Not only will your rental unit look clean it will also smell clean and this will be a great impression and a positive note.

### e.  Carpeting

- Carpeting can be an expensive feature to maintain for a rental unit.  A carpet that looks old, shabby or worn will most defiantly discourage a prospective good tenant.  Therefore maintaining wall to wall carpeting will require you to shampoo the carpet before showing the rental unit or installing a new carpet if needed. If you have several rental units you may find that purchasing your own upright shampoo machine will be the most cost effective.  And if you are handy you may wish to install the carpet yourself. Check out some techniques for do-it yourself.

- Hardwood floors are great. They are the most economical in floor maintenance and upkeep. Also hardwood floors are a popular feature used in a room design.  Many times hardwood floors are treated with area rugs or carpets to become part of the room décor and accent the room furnishings while exposing the wood floor on the perimeters of the room. Area carpets can be supplied by either the landlord or by the tenant.     This is your call and your decision will become apparent after showing the rental unit several times to get a consensus of what prospective tenants are looking for in your area.  There are times a prospective tenant will prefer to purchase their own carpet for one or more reasons.  If you supply the area carpet it is easier to keep the rental floor looking good for a lot less than installing wall to wall carpeting.   Depending on the responses of showing the rental unit with bare wood floors you may offer to supply the area carpet while setting some guidelines for color and price.

- Hardwood floors in an apartments where there are tenants living below are not good. Area carpets, hall runners, or wall to wall carpeting is suggested.

## Smell Nice

### a.  Fresh, Clean, Pleasing Smell

- Now that you have prepared your rental unit and have it ready to

show it is going to smell clean and fresh.  This is important and will also effect the emotions of a prospective tenant in a positive way.  As was mentioned before most people buy on emotion.   You may want to enhance the smell a little by spraying some air fresheners that are light clean smells.  Do not spray any heavy artificial scents as this will defeat the purpose and may turn some people away.  Use natural scents such as fresh air / rain scents /  light floral /.   It is important as to what scents you use.   Some years ago research was conducted on how scents can influence a person in a retail environment.   It noted that when a retail store sprayed certain scents the customers would respond differently.  When the scent of orange was sprayed they note that the retail sales would increase.  Orange was also found to have remarkable cleaning qualities. To review the research on how people are affected in scented environments link to the following websites.
www.rentascent.com,   http://www.scentair.com/scent101.html .

## Safety Features

- Safety is important for several reasons just to mention a few. First safety should always be practiced in everyday life, for yourself, the people around you, and your customers.  As a Landlord,  an inspection of  the property inside and out should be done on a regular bases. Any time you are at the property observe any area that can or may be a safety hazard  and have it repaired, adjusted, or improved whatever is applicable to make it safe for everyone.  Inside the rental unit  the following are safety features that should be addressed.

a.  **Smoke Detectors**

- Depending on you local codes they may stipulate where and how to place Smoke Detectors.  Some municipalities may require Smoke Detectors be placed at least one on each floor and at the bedroom areas and/or one in each bedroom. Please check with your municipality for any local fire and safety requirements in your area.  Smoke Detectors come in several different types, such as  battery operated, hardwired with battery backup and wireless inner connected.

b. **Fire Extinguishers**

- Every Rental Unit should have at least one Fire Extinguisher and be inspected once a year by a Registered Fire Inspection Company. A Fire Extinguisher is usually placed in the kitchen area on the wall that is easily accessible and in plan view Please check with your municipality for any local fire and safety requirements in your area.

c. **Proper Exits with Signs**

- Each Exit should be marked with an exit sign. Depending on your type of rental unit(s) and the local codes you may be required to have Exit Sign(s) that are lit with a battery back up in case the power should go off. Also a rental unit with a third floor living space should have a rope latter for exiting in case of an emergency. Please check with your municipality for any local fire and safety requirements in your area.

d. **Locks**

- All Entrance Doors of the rental unit should have deadbolt locks and must be changed preferably as soon as the old tenant moved out. Do not replace the lock with a lock that was used on another rental unit as this is <u>NOT</u> a good practice. Deadbolt locks are easy to replace. The most inexpensive method for changing a lock is to remove the tumbler cylinder from each lock and take them down to the locksmith. Make sure the locksmith can change the tumblers of the locks while you wait. Most of the time waiting for this service to be completed should not be a problem. Always ask for the old key back so you can verify the changed lock(s). When changing the entrance door locks of the rental unit all should be keyed alike. By doing this it will be a convenience for both you and the tenant. Another way to change the deadbolt locks is to buy a new lock at the hardware store. By using the same brand and lock style the locks can be easily installed by just removing the old cylinder and replacing it with the new key cylinder. The deadbolt itself would not need to be changed because there is no difference between the old and new bolt unless there was some type of improvement made to its style or durability.

# Chapter 4

## Know the Fair Housing Law

*Understanding and complying with these regulations is essential when renting a property. This is a* **MUST DO**.

- **The Fair Housing Acts** prohibit discrimination based upon Race, Color, Religion, National Origin, Family Status ( includes those with children under eighteen, pregnant women, and the elderly ) Disability or Handicap, Sex, Sexual Orientation. The Fair Housing Act is enforced by the Department of Housing and Urban Development also known as (HUD). Title VIII of the Civil Rights Act of 1968 also known as The Fair Housing Acts include The Fair Housing Amendments Act of 1988 as well as the Americans with Disabilities Act of 1990 establishes an administrative enforcement mechanism, provides stiffer penalties than the present act, and expands its coverage to include disabled persons and families with children.

- **State, County and Local codes** may have additional laws and may prohibit exemptions given to small landlords pertaining to the federal Fair Housing Acts. County and Local levels may at times be more stringent than federal or state Fair Housing Acts. For more information on Fair housing regulations for your state, contact your state fair housing agency or your states consumer protection agency. You may also wish to review the following websites to become more knowledgeable with the Fair Housing Acts.

- Examples of discriminatory practices prohibited by landlords can include;
- Advertising, that indicates a discriminatory preference.
- Refusing to rent to a protected class.
- Setting restrictive standards in selecting tenants.
- Falsely stating that the unit is rented or denying that it is available for show.
- Asking questions about an applicant's disabilities that are not necessary or appropriate for the application process.
- Refusing to allow a resident with a disability to make a reasonable modification.

9

- Directing a prospective renter to a specific area or neighborhood based on one of the protected classes, this is known as steering.
- Setting different terms, conditions, or privileges before or during a tenancy
- Inconsistency in the treatment of prospective tenants, such as requiring some to pay larger deposits or rents.
- Terminating a lease for discriminatory reasons.

- Examples of what the Fair Housing Act does not cover and a landlord can refuse.
  - If a person can not afford the rental unit.
  - An owner is not required to rent to users and dealers of illegal drugs. Also note
  that if a person is a recovering alcoholic or drug user and is in recovery and not using they are considered to be disabled and are governed under the disabilities act. The proper documentation must be supplied to verify the person is in recovery.
  - Landlords can set rents at whatever the market will allow.
  - Landlords can apply nondiscriminatory rental criteria designed to evaluate a prospective tenants or applicants character, credit history and reliability.
  - Landlords can refuse to rent to an individual if documented reliable information shows the individual has a history of violent, disruptive or destructive behavior.
  - Occupancy is over the HUD and local occupancy regulations.
  - If you find that the person has a prominent attitude problem such as being to demanding or unreasonable. Make sure you keep good documentation here.
  - If the person is not able to afford all the necessary costs including the first month's rent and security deposit when it's time to sign the rental agreement.

## a. Some Guidelines:

- A rule of thumb is to treat everyone the same including what you say and how their application is processed. Avoid questions or statements from applicants that have discriminating remarks or overtones.

- Establish specific rental criteria and **apply it consistently**. For example:
- The applicant must meet the income requirements.
- A rental application is accurately and fully completed.
- A good credit history
- A good rental history,
- No pets if applicable, - except for disabilities see regulations
- Non-smoking.

- Treat all applicants and residents in a fair and consistent manner.

- Maintain records of all applicants, including written policies, applicant contact forms,
and completed applications. Documentation can be helpful if a complaint is filed and is subject for review.

. For more information on Fair housing regulations for your state, contact your state fair housing agency or your states consumer protection agency. You may also wish to review the following website to become more knowledgeable with the Fair Housing Acts.

HUD - Fair Housing / Equal Opportunity
http://portal.hud.gov/hudportal/HUD?src=/program_offices/fair_housing_equal_opp

# Chapter 5

## Determine Your Rental Rate

- To determine what your rent should be you must first know what it cost to run your rental unit or each unit if more than one. This will give you a starting point.  Second knowing what your building expenses are such as Mortgage, Insurance, Business Operations and Maintenance and Repairs. Third: How does it compare to other units by location, exterior and interior appearance and amenities.  Putting the above three step together will than determine a range for your profit margin.  You should be in the positive range to some degree. If not you will need to address what and where your property is out of line.  If your margin is showing a negative cash flow  the attention usually would need to be addressed in steps "Second" or "Third" above.

- **In the first step**, determining your rent for your unit using a utility cost approach can be very time consuming.  Each utility expense would need to be calculated using a combination of calling utility companies,  using formulas, and comparing pass utility records.  Done correctly it can give you some very good  numbers on the cost of the expenses incurred from a rental unit.  A much easier approach in determining  what the utility costs are to operate a rental is to visit your local HUD ( section 8 ) office and ask for a copy of the    "Utility Allowance " for a residential unit.  Note that it is very hard to impossible to get and exact  expense cost but the HUD "Utility Allowance " comes very close.  Usually the Utility Allowance chart is broken down by:

**1st**   **rental type**: Single Unit. ( Detached )  Meaning the rental unit stands alone and has four outside walls. End Unit  ( Double block or end unit ) having three outside walls. And  an Inside Unit,  having one or two outside walls.

**2nd**  **number of bedrooms** under each type:
            Efficiency ( 0 bedrooms )
            Bedrooms 1 thru 6

**3rd**  **utility allowance** for each unit size ( number of bedrooms ) under each of the three rental types.  The  Utilities Allowances  given are for categories:
                 Heating ( oil, coal, electric, gas, propane )
                 Cooking ( electric, gas, propane )
                 Electric  ( basic electric and lights )
                 Water Heating ( oil, electric, gas, coal, propane )

Water
Sewage
Garbage
ApplianceCost ( refrigerator, range/microwave, window
air, central air )

Note that the Heating cost are in ball park estimates and at times debatable
due to the volatility of heating fuel.

To calculate the Average Rent start by adding or subtracting the cost for the
utility. depending on if the utility is included or not.  Example:

After finding the rent level for your unit, you may consider to charge a little
less and you may have a  long term happy tenant knowing they are getting a
great place and good service with a rent a little less that the market rate.

# Chapter 6

## Setting Rental Standards

Before you start advertising and interviewing prospective tenants write down what is the criteria you are looking for in a tenant that will be occupying your rental unit. Such criteria are the requirements need by a prospective tenant in order to rent your unit. These requirements are called Rental Standards. Some examples of Rental Standards to **qualify** a prospective tenant are Lease Term, Security Deposit Fees, Tenants Income, Credit Checks, Pets, Occupancy, Criminal History, and Rental Application Information to name a few. Please Note; It is prohibit to set rental standards that will discriminate based upon Race, Color, Religion, National Origin, Family Status ( includes those with children under eighteen, pregnant women, and the elderly ) Disability or Handicap, Sex, and Sexual Orientation. Make sure you know the Fair Housing Law before you start putting together your Rental Standards. Some Rental Standards can also be State sensitive so you may want to review your Rental Standards with an attorney before you start your interview process.

**THE RENTAL STANDARDS THAT YOU SET MUST BE USED TO QUALIFY ALL RENTAL APPLICATIONS.** You can not use some standards for some applications and other standards for other applications. This would be considered discriminating and is illegal. You must treat every prospective tenant the same. If you find yourself in a situation that you need to make a business call and deviate from a requirement this would need to be a WELL JUSTIFIED business call and documented. It can not be made based upon Race, Color, Religion, National Origin, Family Status ( includes those with children under eighteen, pregnant women, and the elderly ) Disability or Handicap, Sex, and Sexual Orientation. If you should need to make such a business call you may want to review with you attorney first to avoid any legal problems.

If you have more than one rental unit you may have different Rental Standards for each unit. Also when a unit becomes available again you can alter the Rental Standards but remember once you set the Rental Standards you must use them to qualify all prospective tenants and that all prospective tenants must be treat in the same way.

It is Important to keep documentation on your all rental inquires regarding your available rental unit. This means keeping good records on all inquires about your rental ( phone calls, website search, or any other means of contact ), including all pre-screening, interviews, showings, and applications.

**Some " *examples* " of Rental Standards are:**

> **Note:** Standards are presented to a prospective tenant during the screening process even though it may appear that many of the standards are noted in the rental lease. It would be a good practice to have a list to make sure you have reviewed all standards with the prospective tenant and non are missed.

## Lease Term:
- Lease required
- Month to Month,
- 6 month leases,
- Min. one year lease
- Month to Month extensions are available at $125.00 above the current market rent.

## Security Deposit:
- Security Deposit equal to one months rent.
- Required with a signed lease.
- Security Deposit Return in accordance with the rental agreement.

## Fees Due at Lease Signing
- First Months Rent and Security Deposit.
- First and Last months rent and Security Deposit.

## Non-refundable fees:
- Application Fee. ( if not used towards rent )
- Other Fees if any must be noted.

## Application Fee:
- $35.00 non-refundable fee.
- $35.00 non-refundable fee per person required for anyone 18 years of age and older.
- $35.00 is required for co-signers.

## Application Qualifications:
- A rental application must be truthfully completed.
- All rental application questions are required and must be completed.
- All applicants must be at least 18 years of age.

**Credit History:**
- Unsatisfactory credit history can disqualify an prospective tenant.
   ( If an prospective tenant is rejected for a poor credit history, the applicant must be told and given the name, address, and telephone number of the credit-reporting agency that provided the information, as this is required by the FCRA. )

**Criminal Background Checks**
- All applicants 18 years or older are subject to a Criminal Background Check
- A unsatisfactory criminal background check can disqualify a prospective tenant.
- It is suggested to List the reported criminal reasons the applicant(s) can be rejected such as
   - Any felony conviction
   - Any illegal drug conviction
   - Any weapons charge
   - Any terrorist conviction
   - Any animal cruelty convictions
   - Any prostitution related conviction
   - Any misdemeanor convictions against property
   - Any sex related offense or crime against a person.
   - Other - ( )
- All applicants are evaluated based on information they provide in the application.

**Pets:**
- No Pets
- Pets permitted
- Pets permitted breed restrictions apply;
   Dog breeds not permitted are: Pit Bull, Dobermans, Rottweillers, Chows. Presa, Canarios
   - Maximum number of pets per apartment: One / Two / Three
   - Non Refundable fee $200.00
   - Monthly Pet Rent:  $25.00
- Pet Owner must sign a separate pet addendum
- A  picture of the pet prior to approval is required and /or a pet interview required.
- Reptiles, rodents, exotic pets, or other animals that are ill suited for apartment living and in the  judgment of the Landlord / Property

Manager shall be prohibited.
- ( Check with your insurance company / agent for any pet restrictions or
  insurance concerns )

## Income Requirements:
- All combined monthly income of all applications must equal 3 or 4 times
  the monthly rent based on annual gross income.
- Proof of income must be provided to complete the application process.

## Employment:
- Proof of employment is required.

## Non-Smoking:
- Smoking is not permitted in the rental unit.
- Smoking is permitted except cigars or pipes

## Occupancy:
- One bedroom: Maximum 2 people
- Two bedroom: Maximum 4 people
- Three bedroom: Maximum 6 people
- Occupancy standards may be set by local ordinances. Check with your
  local municipality first

## Guarantors:
- Subject to and acceptable credit rating.
- Must have a gross income ratio of 5 times the rent.

*Quick Review for Rental Standards:*
- **Lease Term:**
- **Security Deposit:**
- **Fees Due at Lease Signing:**
- **Non-refundable fees:**
- **Application Fee:**
- **Application Qualifications:**
- **Credit History:**
- **Criminal Background Checks**
- **Pets**
- **Income Requirements**
- **Employment**
- **Non-Smoking**
- **Occupancy**
- **Guarantors**

## Rejecting a Rental Application

**Web - Link**  How to Legally Reject a Rental Application  ( ehow)

# Chapter 7

## Advertise Your Rental Unit

*Advertising is the first step to link your renters to your available rental. The proper advertising plan can save you time and reach your market of potential renters.*

### a. Advertising Media.

- Local Newspaper
- Rental Websites
- Local Bulletin Boards or Publications
- Rental Agencies

- Before advertising in your local newspaper or publications call their classified advertising department and inquire about the For Rent classified rates. Usually the rate will be determined by the size ( number of lines ) and frequency of the ad. The classified ads are read more on Sundays than any other day of the week mainly because more people have more time to read the paper. But don't just advertise on Sunday it is more cost effective to advertise in blocks of days and a newspaper may give a greater discount when you rerun you ad for another block of time. Determine what you want to spend on your ad also figure that you may have to run it several times before you rent.

- These days the internet is being used by more and more people looking for apartments. By using an Apartment search website you can describe your rental in many ways and in great detail. Unlike a newspaper classified you can describe all your features and show pictures even a video of your property at a fraction of the cost. It may be wise to really corner your market by advertising in both the newspaper and an apartment search website.

### b. Review Your Market / Attract your tenant

- Know what other prospective renters are looking at by reviewing your Newspaper Classified Listings and Apartment Search Website. How are the other rental ads being presented then make yours more attractive. Make sure you do not fabricate or use words that discriminate in your ad.

- Keep in mind who your market is - Getting Good Tenants – right ? --- so design your ad to do just that. Your first line of defense is the way your ad is presented. Good tenants will not mind filling out an application, giving references and paying a security deposit. This will weed out some but not all negligent tenants. Also state some of your rental criteria in your ad such examples as "non-smoking", "no pets", etc. This will weed out others that don't meet your rental standards. By doing this it will prevent your phone from ringing off the hook, getting the tire kickers and spending hours of non-productive time. Review the below information and examples stated under the title Ad Structure to help you create your rental advertisement.

## c. Ad Structure

Basic Information
- Location          ....( The first line in bold letters using the city or section is sufficient )
- # of bedrooms
- Utilities Included
- Rental Rate
- Phone # to Call

Rental Criteria ( examples )
- Pets ...................( No Pets / Pets Allowed / Pets Breed Restrictions )
- Non-Smoking
- Lease term ...........( one yr lease / month to month, use next to rental rate )
- References
- Application Required
- Security Deposit
- Application Deposit

--- *Make your apartment sound attractive.*

Special Features / Amenities ( *examples* )
- Wall to Wall Carpet
- Hardwood Floors
- Back Yard      ... ( also state what is in the yard like, cook out area, fountain, ete )

20

- Close to Shopping District
- Public Transportation
- Washer / Dryer
- Deck
- Island Kitchen
- Air Conditioned
- Fireplace
- Garage
- Landscaped

Words that will Attract ( *can use some of these words further describe special features* )
- Beautiful
- New
- Remodeled
- Designer............ ( Designer Kitchen / Bath )
- Attractive
- Large
- Sunny / Bright
- Historic
- Very Nice

# Chapter 8

**Pre-Screen / Phone**   *Done correctly pre-screening will save a lot of time, money and aggravation in finding that good tenant.*

1.   It is important that before screening tenants your property is **ready to show** inside and out, and that you are also familiar with the **Fair Housing Law** .   Next list your criteria or **Rental Standards** for qualifying a prospective tenant and than post a **well designed advertisement**.   A well designed advertisement will be the first pre-screening  and should eliminate some of the prospective tenants who do not qualify.

2.   Make a list of questions that will be used for pre-screening a prospective tenant when you make the first contact with them, this is usually done over the phone.  Your questionnaire should consist of questions like:
   * First and Last name (s)
   * Phone numbers they can be reached at: cell, home, business
   * The number of people that will be living with them and how are related
   * Ask if they have any pets
   * Ask if they or others living with them smoke
   * Ask them where they are living now
   * Ask when are they looking to move into a new place
   * Ask why are they moving

It is important that you keep well organized documentation on your questions and the answers given to you.  This will help to prevent any legal issues such as discrimination if it should arise.  On each set of questions it is also important to note the Date and time called.  To an effort to eliminate using a lot of paper set up your questions in sets and make copies or you may purchase a forms.

Either before and/or after asking the prospective tenant your questions you may discuss the property you have for rent, your lease, and other details.  Review with them your Rental Standards as this will indicate if they will qualify.   You can also weave through the conversation the details and Rental Standards and note each point that you review.  If the applicant *qualifies* and is further interested you should than set up an appointment to show your rental.

# Chapter 9

## Show Your Rental Property

At this point you should be prepared and ready. Your rental should look clean inside and out and ready to show and also that you are familiar with the Fair Housing Law. Showing your rental unit to a prospective tenant will now be your second screening and an apartment in excellent condition will attract good tenants.

## 1. Set up appointments

- After you have pre screened the calls of prospective tenants from your well designed advertisement begin to set up appointments in time blocks. Set up several appointments that are about 40 min. apart. This will serve to your advantage for several reasons. First, If a prospective tenant does not show your time is not wasted. Second, at times when a prospective tenant observers other prospective tenants it creates a higher demand. Its an emotion if used can be to your benefit. Third, Time Management, to avoid the back and fourth trips to show the rental unit giving you time to do other items on your schedule also saves gas and other expenses. When setting up appointments it is preferable to schedule them during the day light hours. It is a good practice to call several hours before the appointment to confirm they will be meeting.

## 2. What to take to a rental showing.

    a.   Rental Applications, should be completed on site if the prospective tenant is interested in renting your unit.

    b.   Rental Standards a copy of the your Rental Standards as a handout or for review.

    c.   Rental Lease for review if necessary. A Rental Lease should be given out after the applicant has been approved.

    d.   Rental Review Sheet : A Rental Review Sheet is not necessary but can be given to the prospective tenant only as a convenience. This can be used for taking notes during the walk through. It will also have your name, phone number and rental address floor plan, and room sizes

e.   *Oh yes*, and your notebook or clip board. If necessary take some notes during the showing   but after they leave first write down the date and time and all pertinent information you discussed and comments that were made.

## 3. Dress for Success

-   Make sure that your appearance is neat and groomed.   A good appearance together with a   professional manor will be a good first impression to a prospective tenant and typically shows that you are a landlord that cares about the property and about your tenants.

## 4. Arrive Early

- Arrive before the showing to make sure everything is in place and looks presentable. Turn on all the lights so everything  looks bright and all bulbs are working.  Use higher wattage light bulbs but do not excide the maximum wattage permitted for the light socket.  Spray a nice fresh scent if necessary. Open and shades and let the sun in. A bright place gives a good feeling to a prospective tenant and helps show off your unit.  If the weather outside is cold you probably have the temperature turned down.  Set the temperature to a comfortable 70 to 72 degrees.

## 5. The Greeting

- Welcome with a handshake and smile, and introduce your self.  When you show the apartment, you first need to consider that YOU MUST TREAT EACH PROSPECTIVE TENANT EQUALLY.  For example, don't offer one group of viewers refreshments and not treat the other viewers with refreshments as this could be considered biased.  The second group could file a discrimination complaint in that you gave the first group preferential treatment.

- Don't assure prospective tenants that the area is a safe neighborhood because if your statement was a factor used by the tenant to render a decision to rent  and something happens you could be held liable to some degree.  There is no guaranteed as to the status of any  neighborhood as any even the most attractive areas could have a problem or problems at any time.  Suggest that the tenant ride around the neighborhood and observe the area also to park there car for a period of time to further observe the area. They can also check the police dept or online searches for additional information.

- Always avoid any implied discrimination when showing your rental. Never talk about race, religion, color, sex, sexual orientation, national origin, disabilities, age, marital or family status.  For further information please check the Fair Housing Law .

- When you are showing you rental to prospective tenants they may offer information to you  through normal conversation that may be not legal for you to ask. If that should happen you can not use that information to base your decision to rent.  Some questions you may ask without worrying about discriminations are:
- How many people will be living with them?
- When do they need the rental?
- Where are they living now and for how long?
- Why are they moving?
- Is there any problem with there current residence?
- Where do they work?
- What do they do for a living?
- Do they have a pet? If so what kind?
- Are there any particular features they are looking for in a rental ?
- Is there anything on there credit report that could be of a problem?

## 6. The Walk Through

**Presentation Readiness**

- Many purchases are made on emotion of feeling good and fulfilled.  This is considered to be one of several key ingredients.

- Make sure you are in a good mood. If you are pleasant and  feel good about the rental unit it will show and a prospective tenant will pick up on that. If you're excited about the rental units appearance and what it has to offer that's even better.  At the same time do not appear desperate.  By appearing desperate unscrupulous people may take advantage of you and good prospective tenants may perceive it as a problem with the rental unit.

- Be professional and conduct yourself professionally.

## The Walk Through

-  As you are walking through the unit show off and highlight the best features and amenities. Make sure your point out  architectural features, fireplace, appliances, room or closet sizes, back yard, etc, etc.  A rental that looks good with attractive features will generate  good emotions and will generally speak for itself.   Also, if you have your unit ready to show and that it is looking good and in order you will most likely feel good about yourself and again this will show through to the tenant in a positive way.  The most successful  Real Estate Leasing  people are found to be friendly, personable and a people person.  This helps to make the prospective tenant open up and feel relaxed, comfortable and easy to talk with.

- If a problem or repair is noted do not try to hide it rather be honest and let the person know when the problem will be fixed.

-  *If the rental unit is vacant* you may offer the prospects some time to go back through the premises on there own. This will allow them to feel more comfortable to review what they can do and how to arrange to accommodate there needs and desires. Let them go through and imagine what can be done.


## 7. The Huddle

- After the prospects have finished their walk through, ask them to share their thoughts with you. What do they like about the unit. You may also ask is there anything that they did not like.  ( This will give you indicators where any improvement(s) may need to be addressed ) Check if they have any questions and once you have answered any or all questions ask the prospective tenant to fill out and application. Note: all prospects must be treated the same way.

# Chapter 10

## The Rental Application

One of the most important parts of a Landlords screening process is the Rental Application. Here we will proceed to explain the Rental Application process in general. Note, as some states may have state sensitive laws or regulations pertaining to the application process. Be sure to know your State specific laws including any local laws. First and foremost you should also be familiar with the Fair Housing Law and remember to **treat all Rental Prospects / Applicants Equally**. This includes using the same consistent process for checking an applicants criteria to avoid any type of discrimination. Maintain records of all applicants beginning from the point of contact using contact forms

## 1. Presenting the Rental Application

- After the walk through is completed, any questions thus far have been address and if the Prospect is ready to move forward towards renting than the rental application is presented to, and to be **completed by,** the Rental Prospect(s). It is the applicants responsible to complete the application accurately and completely. It should be noted to the Rental Prospect(s) that the application must be accurate and complete and should be part of the rental criteria. In most leases it requires an accurate rental application otherwise it would be considered a breach of the lease.

- Many landlords require an Application Fee and that any person over the age of 18 must also complete an application. This will help to cover the cost to process the application.

- At times Just presenting a Rental Application in itself will deter a some bad prospects to continue any further to pursue the rental. And sometimes the prospect will offer information to you about the condition of their credit report/history or other possible issues. Remember to always take notes ( dates, times, and what was said or transpired )

## 2. Verify the Applicants Identity

- Verify the identity of the applicant by checking the applicant's driver's license. If the applicant does not have a driver's license a visa or governmental issued photo ID can be acceptable.

## 3. The Screening Process

- **This process** will help to determine if the applicant will be a good tenant or is unqualified. Remember that all applicants must be treated and evaluated equally and in the same way.

- **First reviewed** the application for completeness.

- **Next, Review the application** to determine if it meets with and is in compliance with the guidelines or Rental Standards set for the rental such as:

- **Income:** That the applicant meets with the income requirements. The general guideline is 25 to 35 % of the gross monthly income should equal the monthly income.

- **Income verification:** In the standards set for the rental, establish the type of documents that are required or acceptable for income verification such as letter of employment from applicants employer, most recent pay stubs, last year's tax record, and / or two or three most recent bank statements.

- **Pets:** First are pets allowed? In additions to any pet standards and pet policies set for the rental standards there are other guidelines to consider that include, the handicap pet or service animal and are there any pet restriction with your insurance company.

- **Occupancy:** When determining the acceptable number of people allowed to occupy a rental unit the following guidelines may apply.
    - efficiency or studio rental unit ....... One (1) person
    - 1 bedroom ............................. Two (2) people
    - 2 bedroom ............................. Four (4) people
    - 3 bedroom ............................. Six (6) people
    - Also important is to check with all Federal, State, and Local occupancy guidelines that apply to the rental. For example

some guidelines such as with the Section 8 program may require that if 4 people are occupying a rental consist of Two adults, and Two children one male and one female than a 3 bedroom may be required. Also some local codes may use the sq. ft. available in a rental unit to determine the occupancy guidelines.

- **Credit reports will contain** much information about an applicant's creditworthiness. The following are some area of interest a credit report will provide.

- **FICO score**
  The FICO score is a numerical score that is calculated by the credit bureau and is based solely on the applicant's credit report data. The range of the FICO score is 300 to 850. The higher the score the better. Any score above 700 is considered to be good to excellent, a score below 620 is considered to be a high risk. **Sometimes the credit score will not tell the whole story or the full picture**, that is maybe an applicant was late on a payment three or four years ago, or for some other reason. In this case you may want to look at their credit report to further determine the reason for the low score.

- **Credit History:**
  The Credit Report will show an applicants payment history, types of credit, amounts owed, and how payments were made being timely or late.

- **Rental History:**
  Credit information may at times include rental history and court records such as Judgments, eviction notices and more information that is of public record.

- **Debt to Income**
  The Credit Report will help to identify the debt incurred by the applicant. In using this information and the income information verified through the screening process you will be able to determine the debt to income ratio by dividing Debt by Income.

  - **Before a Criminal Background Check** is preformed the applicant must be informed of the criminal background check and must approve of such in writing. A well constructed Rental Application will supply the proper wordage and approval procedure that is  required by the applicant.

- **Criminal Background Check**
  Records should be check in all states or jurisdictions for at least the past two or three years. The denial of a rental can be based on any felony or designated felonies such as ( murder, assault, rape, sexual abuse etc. ) occurring within a designated amount of years.

- **Running Credit Reports**: It is common for landlords to check the credit reports of prospective tenants before approving them for a rental. Some applicants may provide their own report however you have no way to determine if the information is correct. You may wish to run a credit report yourself or have a reputable online company do the report for you. Before you make this decision you must first be aware that it is important on how you handle credit information. All sensitive information such as a credit report is required by law to be lock in a secure place. Usually an inspection and service fee is required by an authorized inspector to inspect the location and system you use. An alternative to maintaining a secure location is by using third party screening companies. Depending on the company of choice some screening companies will provide only a credit score and sometimes propose an educated opinion as to the applicants ability as a renter based on their review of the credit report. Other companies will offer more details and varied price ranges. Later in this section you may review some agencies and services companies that provide credit checks, background checks and more.

- **The credit report will supply** important information to assist in the landlords determination. Noted above are some of the areas a landlord can deny applicants housing under the Fair Housing Laws. For example if an applicant has a history of missed or late payments and a poor credit score you may deny the applicant or consider requiring a qualified co-signer or charging a higher security deposit. If requiring a co-signer you will also need to run a credit check on a co-signer to make sure he or she is qualified.

- **Before running a credit report** on an applicant you must first have the applicants permission to do so along with a *completed* Rental Application. Most well constructed Rental Applications will have the proper verbiage granting a release to the landlord to run a credit check. The applicants signature on this release is need to authorize a credit check.

- **An Application Fee** is charge by most landlords to cover the cost . This fee is usually non- refundable however some landlords will abate the cost from the rent if the application is approved. You should not take a rental deposit before checking out their references and do not take a large amount of cash upfront for fast placement in a rental, by passing any type of credit or background checks.                                                        30

- **Below are some Credit Reporting Agencies and Services** to consider. You may prefer to go beyond just a credit report and run criminal background check and eviction reports to evaluate the applicant thoroughly. Review each of the following to determine what type of report or reports will best suit your needs and feel comfortable with. You may also research the market on your own as there are many agencies and service companies available. Some require a membership fee and some will just charge for the report.

- Experian will offer credit reports from the top three reporting agencies. Experian being one of the top three along with Equifax and Trans Union. This will give you a complete picture of the applicants credit history because some creditors will report to only one credit bureau.

- mysmartmove.com    TransUnion Smart Move is designed specifically for independent  landlords and small property management companies. TransUnion offers a unique on-line features that allow the tenant to be screened online and having the results sent to the landlord. The cost for the Application screening can be managed by the landlord or the applicant can pay directly.    TransUnion provides immediate access to a credit report, credit score, detailed rental address history, national criminal report and more.

- TenantVerification.com    ( Tenant Verification Screening ) is a   Tenant Screening Service that offers landlords  many different services if you prefer a more comprehensive report. Along with the applicants credit check you may request additional information on your applicant such as eviction reports, background checks, liens, judgments, and also provides a national criminal records search and more.

- Citicredit.net     Citi Credit Bureau is a comprehensive online Tenant Screening Service offering services to landlords, property managers, and other in the real estate and rental industry. The tenant credit report includes payment patterns and payment history, credit score, SSN validation, residence and employment information. Other services include but not limited to Eviction Report, Landlord Verification, Employment Verification, Criminal Record and more.

- E-Renter.com  ( quoted statement ) is a Consumer Reporting Agency, and authorized reseller for   Experian, Exuifax, and TransUnion.   We have 24/7 online direct access to consumer and business credit files as well as many other databases for credit, criminal, eviction,                31 driving records, property deed records, assessor records, etc. E-Renter services are used by Individual landlords, Property management companies, Tenant screening companies, Businesses who need employee screening, and Businesses extending credit to consumers.

- aaaCredit.net ( AAA Credit Screening Services ) Offers full tenant screening, including credit report, rental history verification, employment verification for current and previous employment, criminal record checks, and more.

- amerusa.net A licensed credit reporting agency for landlords and employers. Access credit reports, criminal background checks, driving records and eviction searches.

## 4. The Results

- **Application is Approved**
  - Notify the applicant by letter or by Phone.
    - Approval Letter
    - Welcome Letter

- **Application is Approved with Conditions**
  - Requires a co-signer or guarantor
  - Requires a larger security deposit
  - Notify by letter and phone explaining the conditions of the approval.
  - Conditional Approval Letter

- **Application is Denied**
  - Call and inform the applicant personally of the application status, do not leave a voice message. This should also be followed up with a denial letter. If the adverse information was supplied be a credit agency do not disclose specific information from the credit report. Inform the applicant to directly contact the credit agency and supply the contact information of the credit agency that supplied the adverse information. Also, when writing a denial letter be respectful of how you present this letter. Do not use harsh words like " rejected" rather use words like " not accepted', "declined", "not approved" or "denied".

## *Disclaimer*

The information provided herein is not intended to be or construed as legal advice, and should not be considered a substitute for obtaining legal counsel or consulting your federal, state, local laws.
Seek an attorney's advice licensed to practice in your jurisdiction.

## References

HUD – U.S. Department of Housing and Urban Development
http://portal.hud.gov/hudportal/HUD

HUD - Fair Housing / Equal Opportunity
http://portal.hud.gov/hudportal/HUD?src=/program_offices/fair_housing_equal_opp

HUD – State Information
http://portal.hud.gov/hudportal/HUD?src=/states

HUD - Fair Housing
http://www.hud.gov/offices/fheo/FHLaws/yourrights.cfm


Do not have to rent to because:

If a applicant can not produce the proper documents or information required
If an applicant who does not meet financial criteria.

# Chapter 11

## The Landlord Call

- Calling the present landlord of a prospective tenant may not be the best idea. If the present landlord is having problems with the tenant he may tell you good things just to get the tenant out. It is always best to call the previous landlord of a prospective tenant. In able to do this correctly you will need to verify the previous address before calling a landlord . A prospective tenant who is trying to deceive a landlord will have a friend or someone front as a previous landlord and give you an incorrect statement about the applicant.

- First, a well constructed Rental Application is important. It will provide for the applicant to not only supply the present address and landlord but also ask the applicant to supply the previous address and landlord.

- Second, the Rental Application is reviewed and is check for compliance with local, state and federal guidelines and that it meets with your Rental Standards .

- Next, it is time for the credit and background checks.  Most credit reports or background checks will verify the applicants previous addresses.

- Once the applicants previous address and landlord have been verified you may call or write to the landlord regarding the applicant.
- If calling or sending a letter to the landlord some questions you may ask are as follows:
  - Has the tenant always paid rent on time, if not, how many time was the rent late and how many days after the due date was the rent late?
  - Did the tenant maintain the premise in good condition, if not, how was the premise kept?
  - Did the tenant maintain the premise in good repair, if not, what was the damages?
  - Did the tenant ever breach the lease, if so, what was the breach?
  - How did the tenant leave the premises?

- If writing a letter to the previous landlord many times landlords will not respond in a timely manner or just not respond at all. You may have to follow up with a call.

- Sometimes a landlord will be reluctant to inform you for different reasons particularly if the applicant you are inquiring about was a bad tenant. *If this should happen, just as one question...............* **Would you ever rent to this person again?**

# Chapter 12

## The Visit.

A picture is worth a thousand words, and so is observing the real thing. If you need more convincing from the applicant try observing how the applicant lives. Drive by the applicants residence or just stop by and visit. Years ago some bankers before approving a loan would take an opportunity to look inside an applicants car. If the car was neat inside or was sloppy with clutter and junk on the seats and floors as this help to determine the character of the loan applicant and possibly how the loan would be treaded. Yumm,,, what do you think,

Imagine a car without clutter would it showed responsibility, self discipline, good character, along with other good qualities. If the car was sloppy inside with clutter and junk on the seats and floor it would general indicate lack of personal responsibility, lazy, along with other poor qualities as this would make a bad impression and possibly work against the applicant to some degree. Today this technique may be discriminating or not legal to use as a means to make a judgment call however it does indicate a negative impression you may want to look a little deeper.

www.ingramcontent.com/pod-product-compliance
Lightning Source LLC
Chambersburg PA
CBHW041112180526
45172CB00001B/217